MOCK TROUGH RASPING CROW

— ALSO BY BILLY CANCEL —

PSYCHO'CLOCK (HIDDEN HOUSE PRESS 2016)
GAUZE COAST (HIDDEN HOUSE PRESS 2015)
INNOCENT TEETH (HIDDEN HOUSE PRESS 2014)
HEADLESS MULTI VS. PERPETUAL INTERFACE (HIDDEN HOUSE PRESS 2013)
THE AUTOBIOGRAPHY OF SHREWD PHIL (BLUE & YELLOW DOG PRESS 2011)

MOCK TROUGH RASPING CROW

billy cancel

BLAZEVOX[BOOKS]
Buffalo, New York

MOCK TROUGH RASPING CROW
by billy cancel
Copyright © 2017
Published by BlazeVOX [books]

Interior design and typesetting by Geoffrey Gatza
Cover Art by billy cancel
Author photograph by Alexey Novikov

First Edition
ISBN: 978-1-60964-293-8
Library of Congress Control Number: 2017944667

BlazeVOX [books]
131 Euclid Ave
Kenmore, NY 14217
Editor@blazevox.org

publisher of weird little books

BlazeVOX [books]

blazevox.org

21 20 19 18 17 16 15 14 13 12 01 02 03 04 05 06 07 08 09 10

BlazeVOX

Acknowledgements

Much of MOCK TROUGH RASPING CROW originally appeared in the below publications: Altered Scale, Altpoetics, Blackbox Manifold, BlazeVOX Journal, Blue & Yellow Dog Press, Boog City, Bombay Gin, Boston Review, Country Music, Cricket Online Review, E ratio, Euphemism , Ex-Ex Lit, Frigg Magazine, Futures Trading, great weather for MEDIA, Gobbet Magazine, Helios Mss, Hidden House Press, Map Literary, Mush Mum Mag, MV Gallery, Other Rooms Press, PEN America, 'Pider Magazine, POSTblank, Pretty Owl Poetry, Skid Row Penthouse, Streetcake Magazine, The Jivin' Ladybug, The Miscreant, Three Rooms Press, Tulane Review, Unlikely Stories, West Wind Review.

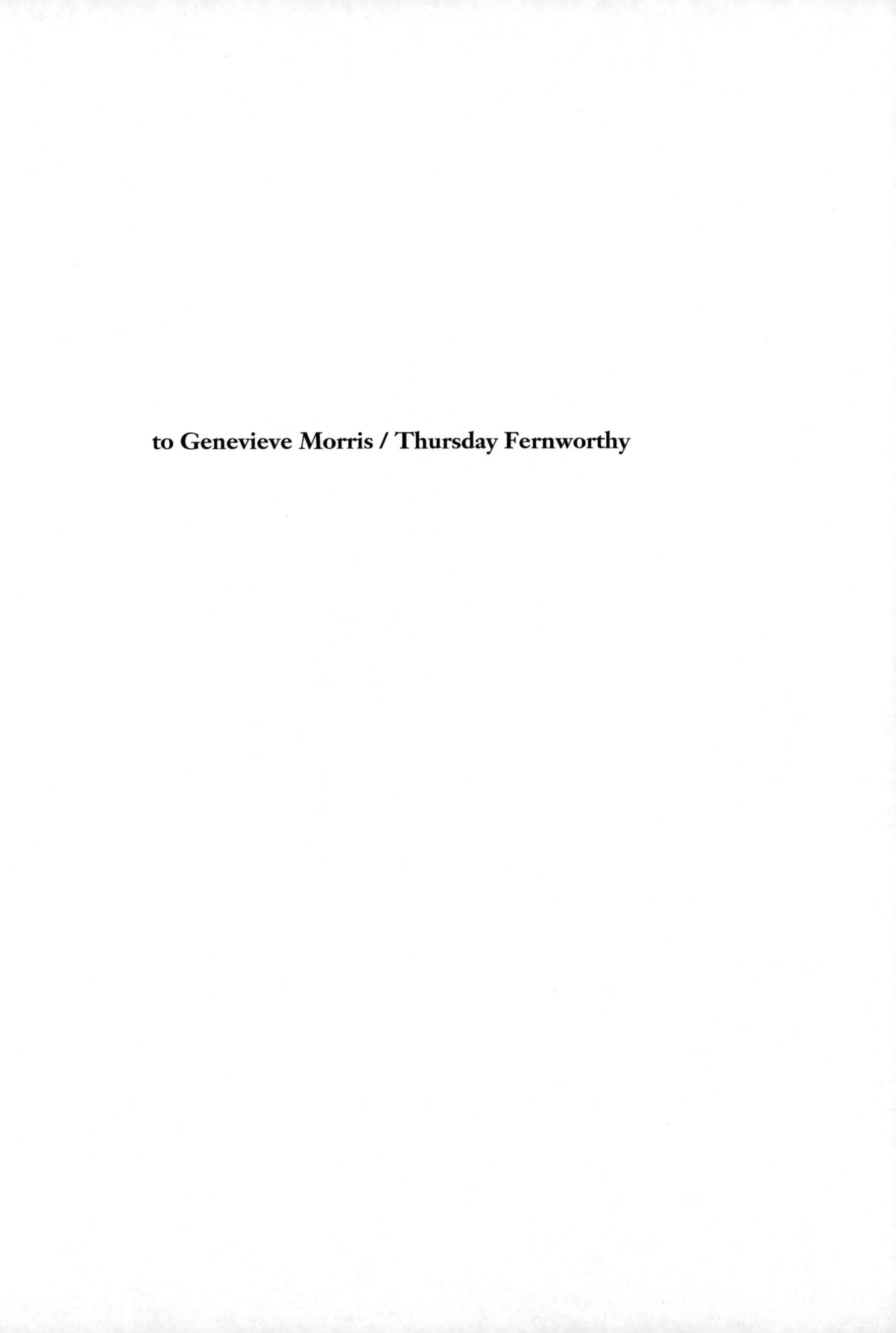

to Genevieve Morris / Thursday Fernworthy

Table of Contents

Mock Trough Rasping Crow

GLEEFUL TOXIC SLOSH MANDATE

born a bit tired in a haunted shithouse
with a sack full of kit   that still needs wiring
up   hence i frequently drop titles of
reference for numeric code   i.e
your bag's open i didn't say nothing is
now   9/21/17 &   gold royal deep blue 9/22/17   but
since becoming a friend of   pedro i cannot go
back to meadow
mayonnaise   extreme close up then   extreme
    angle take   another low octane mascot   lit
up like broadway   is leaning against
the engine because   *collective left*   the door
open   they could not help but
    become tangled up in   the good stuff   which
explains why that layout   across the drink is
protected   by the red blue green with
a key   might yet slip into my roach stompers &
make a swim for it   later in slow town
    rasping gang gets something on someone & if
you want the whole megillah   my ass sucks blue mud

baptized in sweet tea marinated in piss
bad teeth no reason   to laugh less   a gap
in the score for   my specific waste   & though
a candle consumes as   much air as
a man   ain't no average candle   get bits of
lemon for the progress i make   rather
than
biting   man & horse alike   mosquito hawk
    all caught up in the sickly stuff fancies   himself upon a rose
tinged cloud   reeling through space & though   *i'm liable*
to similar episodes this   disregard overture starts
out with a scheme of progression goes   on
to its logical end   the leech moves by
    affixing its rear sucker to
a surface stretching
forward then affixing its
front sucker & dragging
up its rear to begin the
process again don't that
knock ya?

express train fire scene lone fisherman black abstract
forms monochromic field   that's what
we are   mergedowned   tools 'n' gazed
    outsider blue + magic blue   missed this
year's   fantastic entertainment   200 points for
gobbling an insect   body of a man found
off the breakwater   50 points for escorting
you across the freeway   all swirling charcoal
purpose   *monitor the situation*   lamb
    chapter   strip the loop the strip   behind
mobile   this might go dance-at-
which-dislocate-to   because
it has been   territory & our
attention   does
wander   given
    the choice a
long commercial
at the start   no
further
interruption

at horse latitude 4 letter man   recurring motifs
of bread without salt   faulty fuse box means tinsel
orchard held in sudden dimness   red eyed
     from enchanted forest   such breathtaking
display of tomorrow's electronic miracles   really really
scratched his cornea   mutants abounded at degraded
swing dance hall   however he ain't gonna jump
on some prance &   force his way through the push   just
for that   all inmates are referred to as captain   we
     enjoy non-alcoholic beverages   *sat at a table overlooking*
the wild blue yonder   frantic grid tick triggered shin
     collapse which is why we'll be on the pile driver installing
angel creek complaints any?   have
     left white beak in
pink charge until
red light shines   gasper in my mouth daily hate under my arm i am
mouse milker &   this is 0 on my left   you sneak up
behind me however   i'm
warned by the popping of
bugs underfoot

from paint hungry dogleg to day of judgment
you'll be in the midst   of your predecessor's
debris   have to take your cue from   Beast
Master   happy as a high tide clam &
can still go all sewer mouth   when required
to talk up the Big Gate   we debuted the apple
    blossom 2-step around bug house square   didn't
know if it was brazil or christmas   spoke a language of
deconstruction   went bass awkward   1
minute tranquillo next   *reverse lunch*   tried to
sweeten the pot with   some total blow choice   all
fruits ripe &   t'other sider raising hob   then
the main stem broke that was   the thing right &
as i say it happened   would rather be a
    sharply rendered figure   technicolor
skeleton   green yellow nerve
strand   bright flashing
limbs   active available upon
various platforms   than some blow
through dumb fragment

psycho'clock   broiled becalmed   night losing steam can't
be saved by variations of   the serve 'n' paddle
genre or   this city's swift   trade in little
giants   whiskey 'n' cupcakes it's been   waiting for the lord
of the hunt to come deliver the death blow but   ain't ready
to limp   home for   repairs   take shelter in a desolate barn
overnight   angel engine showers unfiltered   pieces of joy onto
    a wide area of dirt white parkland turquoise lake   police later
confirm mosquito nest   is garden of delight   *phew*
    no straggler loss   awake with a hook in my   mouth red
eye busted nose   vinegar means good reputation grog
bad tremors quarrelling the workhouse   next time i'll lean
    from my bunk with a biscuit in 1
hand unwilling   to be prevailed to leave
such a wreck   we proceeded to the end of the stream   tall banks of
    fern   rhododendrons azaleas white pink yellow
scarlet

BLACK crack jags down -
WHITE sky into -
GREY hill

etching 34 - A Dreadful Storm

humash wealth management inc
c.b.d doppelganger   rush of teeth to the head
amidst froth warning   accused of nonsense   even
throughout mercy launch   achingly sour system's
perpetual self-reference   uncouth prefix not woodlands
abound with venison   acorns for feeding hogs   there was
    deep-rooted-pre-established-visual-code so   didn't
have the heart to wake him   in jarring contrast monopolist
hicked spat no one called her up   on her knights
in white satin   loons in white trainers bullshit   ideological
    juggernaut if you think best   plug it in   soon
steel day american fork   so pump up the zeds   blurs
smears a bush to cut a bird to paste   1st pill will relieve
    symptoms of tiredness
2nd pill shall promote
a sensation   like the devil
is about to
come   through
the fucking
wall

celestial navigation for weirdos
yes yes intergrade's limited palette &
don't have much time   suitable
despair backdrop if   you see a spoon in
a cup don't make a joke   bright wash of
     brilliant disregard absolute lack of
community attachment incidentally this
is the point conventional gothic trots
in like an 1000 horse charge & it won't be
worth a single radish   *copy flow break*
     then flick the peter   it'll be all
there in turquoise   purple deep lilac if you see
sharks by day play your radio all night   am
     nothing if not consistent dreamt of a pink
grey cloth patch hill beneath a
blue gauze sky & a single red spot where the
nerve was damaged   if you would like
     an update on the status of
your application at any
time please email <u>ironhorse@alienlandscape.gov</u>

through-BLACK-thorns-GREY-
carriage-GREY-horse-GREY-
sky-WHITE-road
Etching 68 - His Difficult Birth
BLACK lamp above
GREY room-WHITE women
surround-GREY bed / at worst at worst
Etching 70 - Day Of The Animals
GREY beast's licking face
dawn-BLACK figure
GREY bushes
gowanus wholefoods
gowanus wholefoods
brooklyn 11215

FLORESCENT BITTER TINSEL SCRATCH

hey creeping thing   inane echo babble   day
of no contest went   deep shade full
sun cold westerly dismal moan   stow
your wilds & plant 'em   she is closer   faster
than you think   hey creeping thing   avoid
    formative structure   dodge the column   space
for you until   the frosts   *marinate with a poem*
on amber alert   hey creeping thing
    green cabbage or
cabbage green   but
full of stars &
hail   forced to moonshine   thought of a gorilla then
a horse as you   were ground down to powder   ooh creeping
    thing   white thistle   sweet violet   marigolds   so rarely
appear & you've got a throat full of fern & chick filet in your
mouth who are you?   about that time i
    stepped upon   a piece of tin &
it bent & i skated away from there   creeping
    thing   the worm has
not always been   as he is now

cvs goblin highway federalsburg 21632   not landscape
with ruins pastoral figures trees but   2nd biggest retail
pharmacy outlet in the whole damn state   pink-dot-through-
    white-bars warns of messy commute   traffic backed up to
junction 76   for the annual living people their heads
like birds show   when next we meet upon
    kryptonite drive   the light will change   steel lines shadows shall
continually respond   so make sure you keep your egg in morose
spin dizzy $1800 rent check made payable to cockroach
ambassador conversely   each flea has 2 big beautiful eyes
for it has gazed upon celestial vault   in merge-pool-golden-
    age   occasionally let loose *passing train deafening noise*
once trawled up some clubland overstayer   overwhelmed
now with fucking keys   hand out smokes more vigorous
blame work   unprecedented bull market stretch
    means we still have
some bleached
scans of original
left so   charge
your lucky star

in goon principality you   skin of an artist
type who shall ultimately torch motordrome   if it means
emerging king   smoke if you have a stomach
full of mice he'd say   so in a bit i'm popping out for some
fish 'n' chips   red light job so my winter quarters
     fucked   fuse + stitch stitch + fuse while
protagonist shrieks elizabeth refer to
the guidance   *meet me at control alt delete*   i'll be
     the 1 with complimentary silver bag of jet blue airline
peanuts   awoke found myself in front of
some imperious palace   no awoke in the pocket of a
scarecrow amongst rosebush sticks pencil
leads   nowadays prescribe ritual oaths passwords   my
     duties include   dirt bag index   which means working
the shallows   am falsely accused of   preying on game birds but
blossom leaves are my preference in fact   o.d of i-don't-care
     must learn   pay twice   do the ride in reverse   spoiler
alert   this is not some 0-day
effulgent flash note this is
bloody downstream

erased by choreographed henchmen
was the threat   because in hot pink egg
yolk yellow   squandered a month's
earnings thinking about what pleasant   dreams i
could retrospectively accumulate   when
i got back to   armpit of the universe
gouged the surface   sprayed
bright color lines   chipped away at
the face   still a compelling
     alternative to   going down
the turnip field   because tonight
is information moon   & crows are
there   *filling themselves up*   out
     with the captain i dialed   in a mega
dose knew   it would be cranial
disharmony   was up all hours 'til
1 boulder garden involuntary dismount &
now you've gone   all care bear
whispering   where do you think
you are?   site-specific installation? daddy's yacht?   this is the 3-eyed league

when i joined sifter's union blissville chapter   things were on
the slide   much wailing from   between the barges   hotels &
saloons all pulling out   around then kingdom   of slang was much
disturbed by   the arrival of strangers   blindfolded men armed
to the teeth roamed   the capital's streets   insentient modulator
operated upon a cautious   wait 'n' see policy   military firing range
keep out   was referred to   as otter cove   adjoining blue shallows
contaminated silt from the dockyard   choked it   *put that in
your troubadour song*   have sprung from the rotten
    wood of old ships   to receive this fried slice of   trauma raw
in the middle furthermore   much aggravated by these condiments &
excessive seasoning   am peering electric through dark charcoal
orchard blossoms   all dressed for radar with
gleeful precaution against
toxic shadow lapse   only when all 6 trucks filled
with outback pass   may we turbo charge into
soup   the end of the last party i recall
    was heralded by
a series of
gorse fires

boss clown   this formal vanish   is grim
cracked out work   makes me   all the more
reluctant   to switch masters   & my wonky
prism grayed with insects   turbulent smudge
less active charm   my wonky prism grayed with
effort   in a troubling mode   of laugh 'n'
scratch   rock-in-the-box   they write you off as
    some entrance fever conduit   you should snap
a candle turn yellow   fancifully boom yeah show
them   & there's a kid's show for the lot lice   coolly
off-hand artificial   & there's a kid's show for the
lot lice   *anyways back to the long con*   my man
    on the ground   you walk backwards out
of the garden   stumble into blue green yellow
red   shriek don't we all live in the age of
nervous water? sprouting cousins keyed into
the zeitgeist   at the carnival of acronyms   my
    trousers split my tooth falls out   at the carnival
of acronyms   i become
antarctic 10

glass of lunch with some bombsville face stretcher
my 2nd rate hometown is usually   the scene of such
meetings   fair question would be   what's on the rail for
the lizard?   if you find this less than
gross perhaps   you should provide comforting
support because   i'm more attached to
unsettling backlit   places than people   viewed today through
     minus 7.5   but minus 6 would have done   glimmering to the
accompaniment of   *some kitsch orchestral score*   giving
me the terrible urge to strip   back & edit then
shave the muck   am likened to ___ my day is ___ my numbers
     are ___ my color is ___ am adept at ___ can help with ___ representations
of me are   strategically placed to deter retro sci-fi aesthetic cobwebs
floodlit center stage   i could change   black dog   for monkey   but
     your arms & legs   must
be painted on &   we have a name for
people like you   where i
come from &
that name is
king

went marginalia shroving   far from passionless
thugdom   shadow on neighbor's lawn meant
unimaginable bug out   was set upon a detour   took
wrong turn   got told rope cut   from coil   wouldn't get
2nd chance good   knew there weren't a sweet tooth amongst
those grinders anyhow   positive stuff went with it   *bran 'n'*
    mash   no cause for complaint   preserves my temper   lush
datafication has neither been requested nor   shall be well
received   for years have i lent against   sat
upon   hung from   this wonderful clearing   blooming plants
flowering stalks   low key high energy jolt sometimes   cheeks overlap
can't smile wider   etching 24 - Hunters

GREY horsemen - WHITE path -
BLACK thicket - WHITE sky -
GREY trees
    no rites of

    passage catapult though   scattershot prolific   meant
occasional cosmic cut   however ambitions were dashed
lost upon pillow's edge   couldn't find work   so wandered
off into the forest where   i ride a cockerel play
synthesizers & more   often than not raise pigs

BLAST OF WEEDS DOWNTOWN SPURT

ain't chopped liver get the manual
have a face like   a bucket of smashed
crabs   hurting for certain   don't
think about making   a fashion
arrest in this hype joint   have you tried
hospital food? because   i'm feeling like
a bag of string right now   if you don't collar
the jive you'll   *feel the physics*   random
acts of play excluded   rattling about a loose
energy streak   across the river   crazy
    county   pines pines trailer
pines   at choke point less
amazing shape pattern boasts   for this
jitterbug in need of a   drop in the
shannon & no ankle taps   he asks can i
    buy this on the never tick?   to which i reply
does a chicken have lips?   causing that dog
towner to go
beef city   meanwhile
global battlefield

adrift fortuitously or be kept for the pot
don't move into next county   just to be
named get-in-the-box-get-
in-the-box   then
presently thin blue tongues of flame   you'll
have to paint draw everything   not to
mention   update the spine   i remember
     last july warm colors approaching ran   *into*
a swarm of 'em didn't get suckered   extreme
principle of beast intervention   orange yellows
reds much
joy   i bit gamely until   the end you could
at least have sharpened your faculties   that
outlandish rig in parsley soup   as near to
right we were going to get   over here
     they've established a coordinated
system of crud   if you need
to   make a
telescope
with your hand

inhale havoc improvise bloom
take the cubiclesshitty   rigid half-sharp yet
gorgeous derange   now is the time   to call
me mascot   exchanged glances glancing
     blows in backwater with prominent   iron hand thus
your voice seeks   me rough king   3rd stop this   on
     glass line   blow out scatterings everywhere   clearly
some freak take   slow
poison best practice   *quelling*
     stars   for some inflexible duke   is what i
did while my clone   pig headed slack & you   scattered
little burns   top notch vanquish they will say
     top notch   all devoted then   inexplicably
fat   arc of milk   magnetic purge   for every
     broken port each insert cryptic   fleeceful
of mouth   mud consequence   post-little dawn alba
assault   am flushed with decoy
loading the
parrot with
echo

advance man came back irredeemably faded
said   my soda vigil at   piss scent post was
subject to   much repetition   noted dark
objects   that suddenly moved   reddish
mice   emitting snort-bark combo   reddish
mice   stitched 'n' stretched 'til i went
code pink   funny as a box of
worms   casual transient she could   do it all   pilot
    celestial   electronic   dead reckoning   distorted
but   never a ripped curl before cut
water   with semi-automatic smile   of a
dislocate   often seen amongst   *backscatter*
sea bed crap   so keep a bright look out
tenderfoot   all this is reflected in their territorial
    markers   personal bubbles   unvarnished
harmony   quote our   intuition tells us where
what color   how much   pretty fast though
& not   particular about
what we
eat

encrypted in the droppings of a crow
some year of jagged
energy   deglaciation on
    the dance floor   but plausible strain means
perpetual fault load   keep trying to
this very day to attach myself
to technicolor fields with
barnacle glue   often necessary to dim a smear than experience more glitch
talk   *timber from some devastated shore spread everywhere*
but does this rushed happy ending really
ring true?   i thrilled to
    the terror of the beast with 1000 eyes while
you had the
audacity to
pick
berries on
the hillside &
return to
find the
village gone

as sure as flying saucers make an annoying high-pitched whine
when they emit   lasers   my grace curdles milk   worse
mimics the thwack   of a paddle against   some plastic ball
thwack   once cattle fat 'n'   drowsy brought me cake as i
    sat in the shade of   a cedar   sound walk followed   disappointing
clunk rather   than resonant boing   highlight was   shouting at
a creature   so it moved swiftly to   some nearby hill   myself i fled
stingray city to escape the   *fuzz gauze praise of men*   dallied about
incommunicable space besprinkled   with unknown threat assured
myself   scummy bucolic lay beyond echo bridge & today have been
proven inconclusive   etching 32 - At The Bottom Of A Deep Ravine

GREY slope - WHITE
ditch - BLACK thicket -
GREY sky - GREY stars

     on the plus
    side   cloud of gnats 'n'
flies has just sent me a   friend
request &   all other
earthly
things
pale

quirky unplaceable distress signals   rusting
orange salmon pink   because firewall blocked
captain swing letter twitter feed &   rotten borough
arts scene was too much based   upon wobble head at
the clack shack blue lamp disco   had a pocket of
fews & 2s   got added to the wreck pattern   then
insinuated into   some dialogue   pushed out upon
    a boat   pale white sunset   long streak of
misery   *gave me fixed*   coordinates as   obtained
from lighthouse   buoys &   pier lights   reached some
common space baited with mirrors fell in   with owl
shit junction fish 'n' chip mob   all colors regimented
to contested landscape   what best you come
    for?   to break all the machines to bits?   no
for joyous rollicking pretty little dales small green hill or
anytown u.s demolition party   & ain't the beer cold?   in
    2017 i wrote 48 poems 4 a month in 2018 i intend to write
1 poem 48 times   see you around campus   see you on
the costa del sludge   see you where
the crows fly backwards

was taking a walk for pleasure blue notebook
my approach untypical   some events i connected
triggered a formation blew a crooked road
straight   harmonious progress through west
    barbary   but am now confined to my bed for the
whole day   having been pelted with stones   warmest
regards billy cancel   recollection of another long 1
    in hazy lush data dump a remarkable drill   bramble
status at ice mast &   low bramble status   occupants
of the deep cut   teenage blue mock machine
deluded black sticks   deluded fat fingers   were
they ropes?   forever carriage this spot billy
    cancel told me   conversely this is our attack   very
much a surprise to me   to find us standing here in
view of *vivid red fields*   disguised as
unattainable creatures   you managing a labyrinth just
off the southbound junction to dark summer collapse
me wandering russiamerica counting prostrate
figures   at institutional convenience   we should goldleaf
    sunnyhillboy   break hacksaw's teeth   rainbow about

upending the medium | after 2 glasses of
skirmish it's | easy to negotiate | vicious
coral heads | from the cross-crests | & openly
grapple with the | problem of staying
totally over | groomed myself for
the crust | down to the rivers | at
professional slack meister scene | with by
chicken dance | night after quite
banal | irritating scaling up the micro
actions | choice
another | perhapser in | struggle valley
one pot swerving about | the joint | it's
money or turd with me | sometimes get
followed through the covering | dar
a pack of | hell bounds with | fiery tail
will-o-wisp style | am the most po
known | to man | 507 billion tim
brighter than the sun | some
basic facts from | an obscure li
zealous thresher | village b
ed to | pink so | glad we | were ca
rang for | slack ebb | cou
now | back to the farm |
ong is only in effect | 2 hou
ide | or else | it's the sky
ign | or the block 'n' fall
less red in markings | i've returned from the
shambles with a fresh fresh horse | so check your
this sounds like | a personal problem | they're b
from a fool's errand | with a club fed lobby pass &
acid tea jeans | well up for craptitude swoon
time | spud & onion man declares he's also
got the warm fuzzies | for a

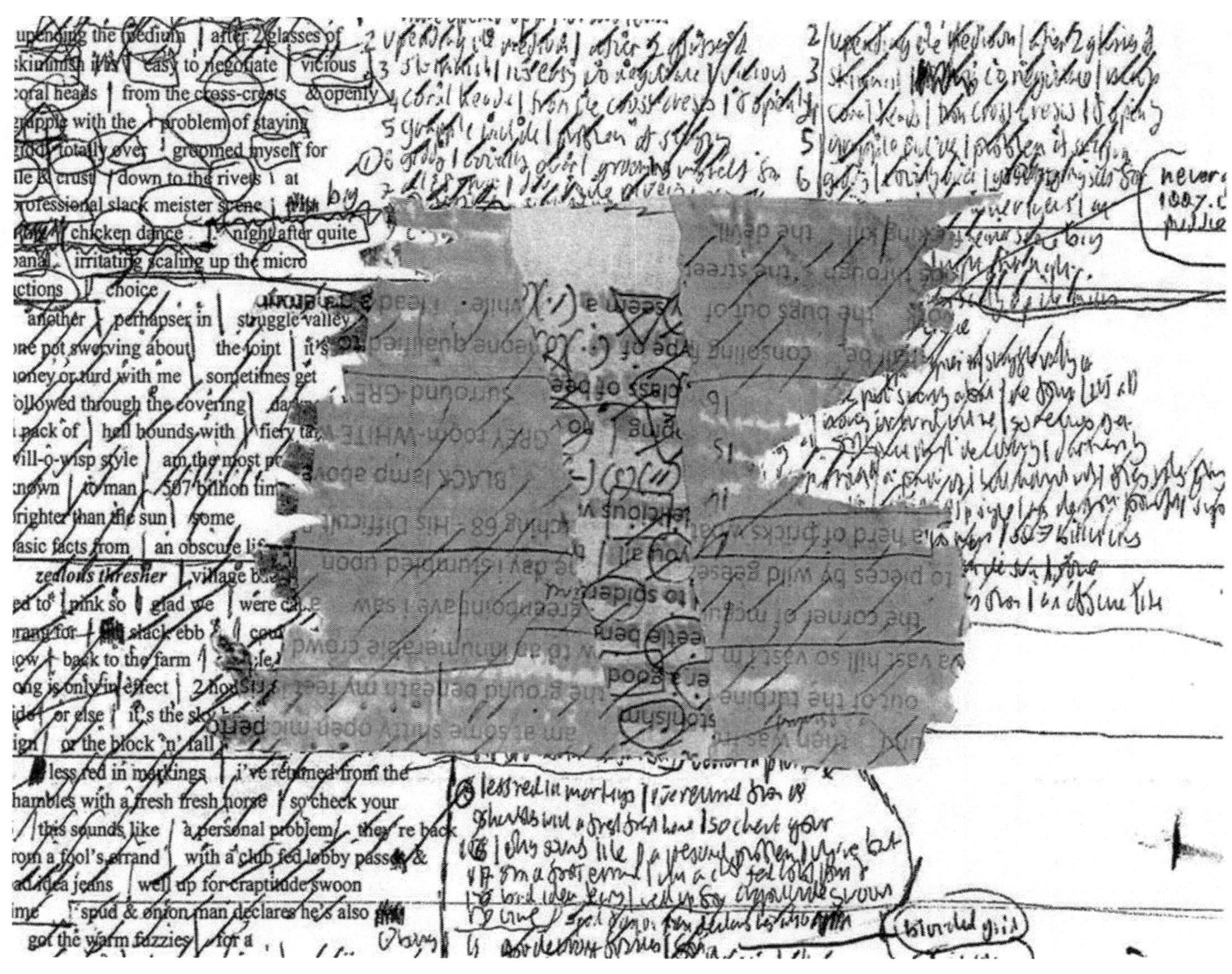

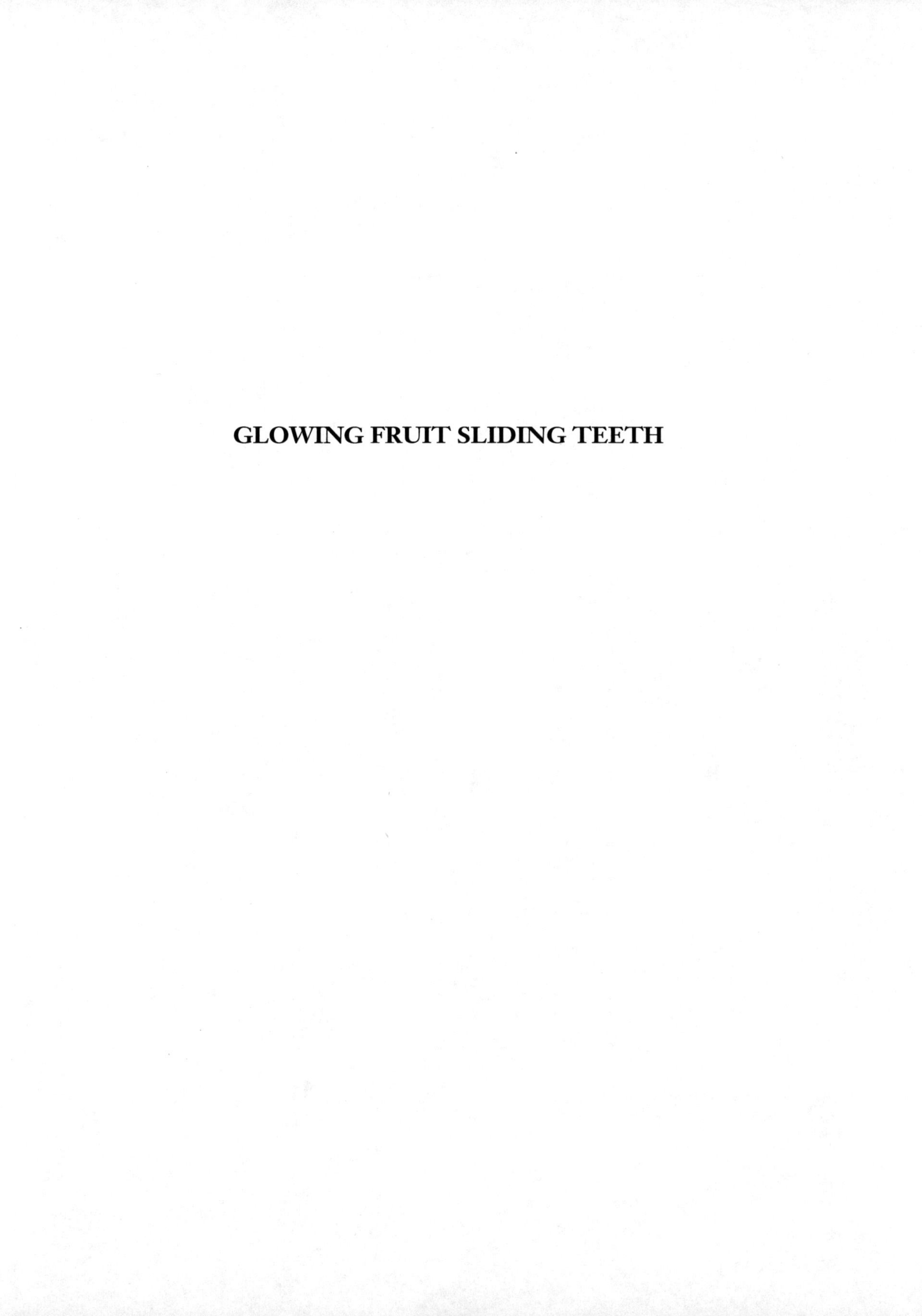

GLOWING FRUIT SLIDING TEETH

in the event of fire we will all hang out   same way   we tolerate
shade better than most grasses   repeat pink pills for pink people
no man has ever become suddenly   though very green studded
with wildflowers   this venue is a total receptacle for shitty kids menace
to navigation race to the bottom mistaken for lunging central   well
    it's been another day of boyish work at the quarantine center behind mind
numbing complexity psychedelic sweetness machine has been going shudder
bang thud hiss spewing bolts for days since   i put a steam hammer to some
potato bugs &   *suffered from convulsions no*   affair of starched white excited
squeals this   etching 12 - Taking Shelter On A Country Walk

through BLACK thorns - GREY

clouds twist - BLACK flock -

town tiny WHITE

                                                for sleek
    in credit brutals   accessories on the rampage   follow   full
blast sun cult   myself am bawling vulgar
sermons to some jeering crowd   would love nothing more
    than trance cramp trance cramp trance at the center of some
weed choked season   but through a gash
in the cargo wall i see   clover leaf intersections
overpass tunnels elevated highways flashing by

this is milk hill that was ragged annex
chronological now   through apple-scab
mandate hunting   then gathering about
dark blue black green miles   of slip cover
you guessed those distressed signals didn't
come from syrup table   but from steep
black cliff face tiny blue light climbing
& drinking   with thoroughbreds helps me
forget   am blue capsule on black red
     capsule on grey   please excuse the pencil
i have to start everywhere rosewater sloshes
about the iron lung what the hell was your
status level pre-robbery?   am pink capsule
     on wood wooden capsule *in the king's head*
no one remembers us   a shadow leads a figure
around the old phosphate plant busy night for
rescue services   am blue capsule on black
     red capsule on grey
i have to start
everywhere

neigh-on-baltic here in land of twang
& milk the suck   is a must job now   am all
over the character academy like   some mad
guy's shit   with my trademark formal
exploration   much into
off-brand cigarettes   for this area code
bean feast   courtesy of your host   never-
wasser   if you have the blahs   *replace*
distance with
a notion of
range   what sort of
    day will this be considering it's so far
been shapes slowly meshing spreading brightly?
& though i'm mindful irregularities
resonate
louder by accumulative effect careless
parry by   simple ringworm gets   me
messing with nature then   can't hit a lick   another
    puzzle factory little
end   of nothing

hometown castaway eyes leaking blue
high over gauze coast with
a gutful   yeah   an unusual brightness
to that   place below where i drew men
horses other things i liked   got
seduced by gangrene   am still
patiently awaiting my   retrospective
nick name revision   do you wanna go somewhere new?   yes   then put 2
    contact lenses in 1 eye none in the other   while i threaten you with
schism between content & form   my fledging
attempt to avoid scorpion riddled holes   while
gathering 32 magic coins in a
frantic 20 minutes was subdued by jackdaw havoc   *dazzled*
snag novice with   half-slope then jackdaw havoc   unremitting sequence of
all devoted until jackdaw havoc   when you gonna begin vague sugar?
after jackdaw havoc   sometimes the claw rather than the nail would
    have done spark marshal   that tight default   radiated some grace
upon our brittle spectrum   hey billy it was great to meet you & see you
    desalt the herring   i run a monthly series at liquid split called decay
night would you like to read?   yes

56

crank up the pig foot   dazzle kid
rough few   incident stream
marigold crisis   now
grey drift   take me   to my
pipe   before the skim 'n' scum
arrive   of their
    spectral puppet play you
must trace their
cunning wires   & leave
this woodsman
little to say   cryptic signage but
unfettered by such nonsense let's
go all non-chronological lapse into
self-aware   it must suck being
    you a spokesperson said   to which i countered fresh proliferation upon
sloping grassy margins is what it's all about   *eels is snakes*   we know
    that   but here is   the recipe   take it for
what it's worth   at home   before
slagging
it off

burstnorms were not icarus-in-blue-hell
1st 1 i met   last 1 i felt retroshock
retroshock   by logic of dominion wilderness
they were mingling   with a storm's clamor
raging wide of hermetic code's   fractured informed
makeshift habitat   state of exception   p.s
    stick your head in this hole   dazzle camouflage
black yellow lines   dissolve reassemble
into an infinite series of relations   *not*
    dazzle camouflage   1 of my signature dance
parties   jack-o-lantern north brooklyn ward
elegantly daunting obstacle course for oafs 'n'
claustrophobes   wise man said only fools
rush in   but i couldn't help losing all urge
before i reached retroshock   funk
    train wrecks both
sides of my mouth   at the same time well-honed
contemporary strategies   deep in the 5th
season from close red
orchard lunatics gawp

had eyes like piss-holes in the snow
through desperation hour   eyes set at 8
o'clock during the grinning contest   it was
another day up the king's ass   searching for
the clean upshot no clean-up shot   landscape
resistant to striving   controlled line & drip
aspirational at best   with the very sounds of the
tavern going on about me   realized was drinking
at the trough but   when devil's half acre shows
in my kill box   *& i am full of beans & rage*   someone
is going to get a dry shave   so don't agitate the gravel
mock-litany man   fierce properties   gentle
     perspective because i know you   had some but
the wheels came off & all   turned to custard   so
this is a gentle retelling of a
familiar yet   multi-layered
narrative   there is a 3rd man   open your face let's
     blow this piss ball   oliver is in
town   osmosis
amoebas

a 3rd team of white oxen & angels plough alongside us
beneath sucker state's mad canopy   no intentional slapstick as
yet thank fuck   tectonic-summer you were there   powerless
    structure you were   recall in the precinct how   we're only
transmitting shopper's aggregate data meant reassurance?
    too sweet for minimalism   too hard for pop   even in
slumberland   this fragility triggers aggression   which is why
i'm on the pile driver right now installing   a cushion wedge   songs of
    grace proceeded to make   overcautious formal choices   i.e military
lamb dead wheel & i sat in winter clay works   heard dumb
shapes screeching   agreed there was a sourness here
        appropriately an ancient free standing celtic cross marks
the site   *this is a good year fruitful in woods & field*   but
sorrowful with pestilence   the usual spring of water appears
at least   can't beat it   at deep seam academy got outfoxed
    sizzled in   our own pattern   storm   a lesson in perspective
dropped the ball in a building riddled with listening devices   if
    yellow black horizontal blocks   fill-freeze the upper tier   i'll burn
driftwood down along the creek   until the sun is lost behind the
trees   & polka dots diagonal silver lines web the clean middle

DIGITAL RIVER ZENITH BLOCK

***to that clusterscrew take the ankle express**
if you need your batteries charging   flash-
jack-new-target   shall be there   kicking a
yellow dog should anybody ask   if aggregation
of fragmentary objects   is your thing you
could do much worse   tipsy fending off explicit
undesirable predators seeking   *a reaction*   our
     scrambling descent   improvised technical feat
anonymous transient blur across drastic tones dramatic
misreadings   was all
too luminous
dense   to be exhilarating an opinion shared by most
historians   ain't going to act the wet dog   like
     some biscuit class around-the-way boy   & boil my
cabbage twice   bright shades punctuate our
thought-out compositions anyhow   this celestial
body needs some
gas & we are in a
fit of
mazes

throughout diapause   noted songs of kids
playing in the street   rope walk tightened
over rainbow spring park   grace
default   facilitated spark   radiate
select   you've marshaled aircraft got some
     moves   so prove it in the
face of blank glowing marquees   wet
     myself   in consideration of aluminum cloud   hubble
bubble chronic   through desolate stretch
of downtown   engine was brake   at liquid split
engine is brake   *please brittle don't*
be hard   do you want fog
fruit or would you rather eat decaying organic
matter with the dads?   my spectrum full of
     space coast & you 2 cats
2 laser pens fashioning collisions   grudge
     sample contains toxics spurts
bright color patterns   we're neither
bird nor quadruped won't
be attending the party

blue jab because   no doubt   sorry solicit advice
don't your neck   for slow train blockade
not countercurrent yet   somewhere across burnt
     purple default   monsters review your work in
zero sum   but booing struggler there will
be other opportunities to apply for
internship   continuous shifts   shedding thoughts
     ecstatic mirage sequence   when it came
i broughtetris
i dreamtetris   outspoken
     satellites dressed in early
blue hours track broad attack formations all
through green thursday & greet each other wanna
split it? wanna split?   beneath
     the mask
bacon metal a
stereotype in hard news
taped knuckles i
still bore through
steel doors to reach you though

went to bed a baby goth awoke a barking head
with both hands   i grasp   the whoosh generator   my
jagged mouth complains   of tight lips   while flanked
by a rotating cast of zilches   it is that kind of   stand-
off   who are you? because   i am fun brash a little
nasty   undermining any   transgressive force   ahead
    of the curve   at least   past incidents smoosh together   zany
cartoonlike   it's my pleasure   to reverse flood of
perspective monotonous flow   you can
keep your contortionist &   *mummified devil boy*   7
flexible legs   can't be wrong   not selling out crossing
    over i will   employ a hard-edged geometric
language with   less colors totally actor proof   i shall root
about grasses chewing scenery   out back
shall be a compromised
landscape   where we may
trot-lope-gallop   blank
mirror constructivist
performance   is what
i aim for

& before me an inroad of assholes   a similar game
i tell myself   is being played out   in dense edit   all
delicate pattern shifts   but lofty praise nullified
hair shirt irrevocable   am ready to be cut   into pieces &
self-affix into   a new scene   the alternative being little
white squares that   can be moved smoothly
around   *another day on magnesium*
avenue   ugly buildings across the fence drizzle
me 2nd guessing the institution   was
     horrified at protruding enclave   when
your performance was   done the rush of   sycophantic
multitudes but still i love you   etching 18 - Passed At Night By The King

through BLACK thorns - GREY
carriage - GREY horse - GREY
sky - WHITE road

     eyes

     yellow cake shaped have done
my community service for   laying
a basilisk egg &   comic parallel is
undergoing maintenance   won't be
in operation this week

in cloud basement you play hard ball & chicken   meanwhile
like crap through a goose i go   from cubicle to apartment
stocked with unsettling details   montage of black 'n'
white images follow   anonymous bric-a-brac mostly   as i
sit awkward awaiting noise & light   & watch with the sound
down   as you bumped up   to the lead   chase a phantom
stag beyond   the dark sizzling sun   all this in just the 1st 7
minutes   seeing the greatest   cars in the world destroyed
doesn't compare   at dreg rendezvous when
    the big picture got small   on-screen graphics showed my pink
pixel heart   breaking   was time to gain the friendship of
strange men as the custom prescribed   tech nerd block
little pixel chap came saw me   we bounced
the 1st 4 letters of his name   _off against_
the database   slap a network code on this &
    call it a multiplayer son but
they won't engage your   if
you can't beat it blue
print   these
angels are tired

123 *this smear founded upon radiating blotch*
skewered rampage   meticulous
abandon   skewered abandon   deferred insipid recontextualized
essential   i floated through convalescence   exemplification
spin   floated through   ballistic moonshine contaminated
blossom   hardly a biscuit trip   at theatre of science
     was out of joint   mimetic representation   didn't know
wind picked up chlorine leak   vagaries pulsed something about
future abundance   remember me i tried to turn off chemical valve
either way turned this room bright pink it is today   undercut
     by some uncommitted double   your worm eaten ships coming
apart   so come on all you crazies   *ferry leaves in 10*   that was luke
     warm with   ferals vs. imports 1 of my
favorite artists out of the short-lived
cancelburg haze core scene his new
album pitched camp with swine is
out on frost surf & you can catch
him live on the 22nd at
g spot supporting i kind of
do performance

escape from cat village   remote coastline major
urban center don't care   if it's because i have
the audacity to display distinctive blue markings spread
all over my head   raw obligation stuff   totally
in the wrong ocean   over spilling pink   from
aggressive sliding purple reds   do you know what
i am craving? nothing   quite in its usual
functional
spot   even months into
    capped noon crown-of-throat won't
what irritation triggered   blushing at cake
    central   no explicit game plan   don't want
to tempt bait   *we're all in the same*
bait   recall avocado grass emerald   i stuck
    bits of fern to it   until crowd
rose as 1   chanted
my zip code   you are fresh encased in
    silver foil suggesting this is
screaming uptown bright sloppy but if fuck-thud dents
our summer mask it'll be hair in the butter either way   hair   in the   butter

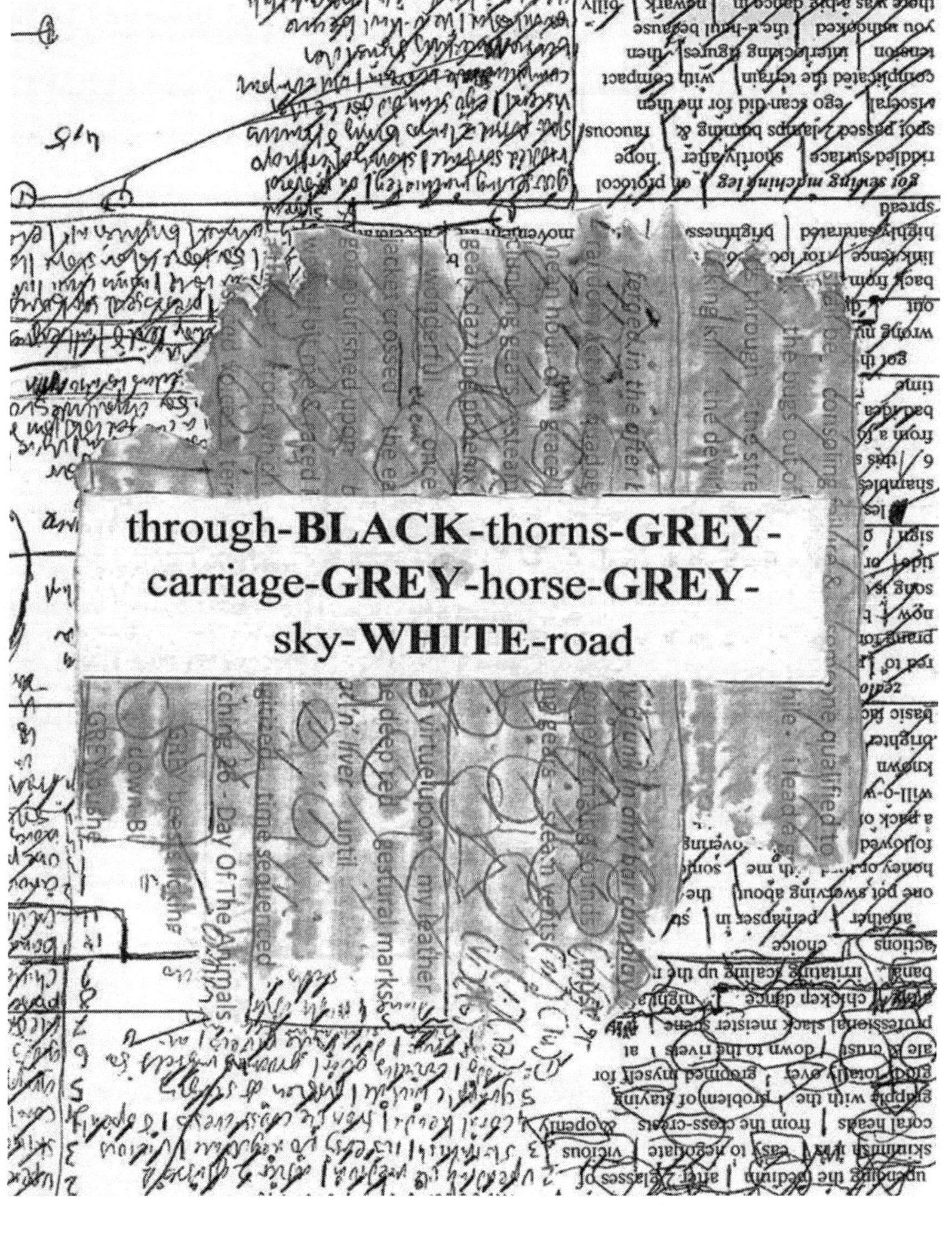

through-**BLACK**-thorns-**GREY**-carriage-**GREY**-horse-**GREY**-sky-**WHITE**-road

THORN CASCADE SPLIT THE GROG

data recovery from a cat's gut
your toneless descending cackle   cold
blooded found subtleties illustrate   bad
milk salty   food   the price for
escaping   a bite charge   my hope is
    that the long awaited 3rd installment of
this clastroepic will appeal to those new
to the genre while not alienating fans
of the original   without due   deliberation
    dense   reeds met open
water   *was hard to*
maintain ascendency   soft
nasal moaning you   would call it   trying to synchronize with
    other   insects we'll have to accept their
strangeness if you step on
an ant it'll go
all indecisive   walking forest roads
    foraging open fields   when
alarmed i hiss   the whole place
star-crossed

why does noise always come from elsewhere?
can it not tolerate waterlogged soil & prefers
sensuous abandon to anchoring in sea grass?   because
      of green green peas blue prince was   smiling yellow had
finally killed what was killing him   potatoes in his mouth when
the 3 blue lights shone   when the stew is on
      the table i'll be in a strange country unused to
the insects best regards the latent hostility
of your chosen medium   but
      with technical fault
load   *our hobble is*
spiked so   when yellow
oxen block our   dead
wheel plough it'll require
more than
a cursory   YOU'VE BEEN TALKING
     ALL THROUGH THIS WHY
DON'T YOU FUCK OFF HOME &
WATCH YOUR
HULU PLUS?

forged in the afterburn of a game any drunk in any bar can play
random acts of quadrupedality   in dingy corners zinging sounds   must
mean hour of   grace is at hand   clunking gears   steam vent
clunking gears   steam vent   clunking
gears dazzling phoenix multicolored
wonderful   once edified by   similar virtue upon   my leather
    jacket i crossed   the east river   got deep red   gestural marks then
got nourished upon   *birthday mutton fat 'n' liver*   until
weasel bit me & raced into   a thicket   from which
emitted digitized   time-sequenced   vocoded   beat-
sliced voices terrible voices   etching 26 - Day Of The Animals

GREY beasts licking face
down BLACK figure - GREY
bushes - WHITE rocks

yeah
    we're both taking   turns regaling this vulgar rabble following   us with
accounts of how bramble
footpath leads onto thorn
road   however while you'll be eating shit at around
    5:30   angels will carry my soul to   gowanus wholefoods
214 3rd street brooklyn 11215

__thus idiocy renews its lease__   plain bold
legible hand   trend follows   signs
off   with groovy red heart   cute yellow
flower   against cracking washed out
background   scratches glitches accumulate
where once was compact energy swirl eye-
popping assortment   guardian of
forbidden sites don't mean space critter
future landing site   johnnies-come-latelies
exclaiming hidden magnet   poem
     the wasteful way you are usually   made   *from cheap scraps*
toothsome dainties   items that drop inside make a funny whirring
sound   often congregate round   flowering
trees depending   on the blah blah blah &
assimilation thereof   banjaxed with color music
     blares from my chest   i wear wonder
woman head band boots 'n' cape   on the
street nice weather   springing through hazel
bushes   outside of work i carry   skunk
cabbage & water bottle

__you beat all round the bush for electronic crop__
whole time under fire from   stakeholders   focus
groups   radio phone-ins   & your mantra of that summer
eased with dung?   white blossom   each dawn   at
control tower north   black mayo upon the tide
line at dusk   was a bad year   for service industries   nickels
dimes
through the cracks   sunday at dusk   means football
     hiving across the land   rope i spin for some bitter
perennial   waiting on the clock   & glue factory to call but
with what gifts you're plagued   back nearest the trough
hands full of flag   inner epic   bracken background   ear
emerging into   the spot reserved for eternal florescent   1
     cyber
monday jack the giant having nothing to do built a
hedge from lerryn to gridlock   my 32nd email from
melancholic fleet read little CIGARS   between the ACTS
become the ACT   each JOY time-based triggers   an ACCOUNT
my problem is   i don't know WHAT to stop   btw the scene of last
     month's fatal pile up   was known to authorities to be prone to fog

sirloin this is shin talking   as sure as
reshuffle proceeds grid collapse   symmetrical
floral patterns do circle these days of jaundice   disclaimer
not all moonshine is worth the elbow grease
1ˢᵗ year more or less like a box supposed
to fit into itself but went like a bad shave
2ⁿᵈ year was all about trying to levitate
a plastic cup   would rather waste
energy surveying mouse damage at the bottom
of the sack   *than hear   another   classic   vanish*
account   call me you say &
     hand me your card with
contact details for
some 24 hour armed
response unit i realize
though you seem to float you're
tethered in fact to
some
intricate
leash

this radar is going scratch 'n' sniff   obtaining all
bronze makes me dopey   just winked
at a strong man   rented an apartment   oh sacred
city of threshold troubadour masher   risk taking
behavior because
nuclear stockpile on your doorstep   charlie
    horse   in summary   gnawed the top off saved
you some   for when twirl slows
up   steady breathe silvery
glow meant   *something snagged getting looped*   frogs
sprung from the
mouth of the host were
a sign of
the filth inside   shall endeavor to
    convince the good people of johnson & its
vicinity of this next friday when i show dressed as
a leopard to receive my garbage
plate then shake my
fist at a sky full of
gizmos

charged by a black knight red pig frosted tree
cave-in tempo   sharp orange place   default
knife clarity   why didn't you give me the time no
    count when i gave you the time?   was rain in upper
peninsula   same day i gained better understanding
of debilitating injury   at the center of an edgeless
    trench   salted their honey traps   within a restless of
shades   half felt the chicken switch   fuzzy laser
liquid home   a road to the right opened up the whole
    of former derelict clay country but green men moved
about the hedgerows   didn't
like it   blocked by a frosted
    knight black pig red tree   naples
in summer isn't now   *such*
a dance is a brisk limp   the cop
in the park at night is you   attracted
    by the noise yellow
fin tuna   2 meters long giants
of the sea are making straight
for us

SACK-WITH-ARMS DEFT SLURRY

help me defend fruiting shrubs
from other distortion foggers   they
provide no results   cacophonous-mishmash-
as-general-strike perhaps   because matter is
out of place   snigger   by the
    radio mast you hang out all day &
translate its   rapid 1-syllable notes as
hey dad   throat of wolf   bear's claw
block block block   see here in
frigid torrid zone if   it ain't 1
madness it is   another   cackle   at the
    zenith of that infatuation   *we were*
okay but   they were in countdown
gouging rump to   flog as steak   because
matter was out of place   guffaw   didn't
    claw through bedrock   just to abscond with
the peddler   early 1 morn   have
flown out to   pluck fruit from
twigs back in 10 &   you are worth
12 acres of standing corn

__i am clifftop false light you are pistol meadow__
do not light chimney   because jackdaw nesting rather
march into toadstone flying   colors banging drum   you've
been duck-egg blue since   horse charge backfired since
hook wind snagged poor sound usage at non-
alignment hot spot   wrote my own
    ticket ascending   sucked up daffs midway through
crestfallen spring   shamefaced bluebell
drop out   experienced slight
electric shock   ripple fault   brilliant headlights no long
sought harvest   if tufty weed-ridden slope to water's edge unchecked
    drop-apples must wake me through my iron hat
does your cup overfloweth with star
soup?   no with
critical distance   golden
    handcuffs buttermilk hill was promised throughout
Prefix Complex   *pushed through brambles furze 'til i*
was   blue mouth purple face   all mood no meat   shouldn't
have got all razed up   for distilling blaze fire   impounding stream then
too histrionic   at terminal curvature   we were joined by a strange huntsman

swivel eye declares   pork all round the
pig's ass   that don't rotate me much
smear-press-spray-drag   are you
going to self-described undersurface?
because   in sweet air   turnip snaggers
annoy the fuck out of me   unedited reality
slice not my idea of escapism   & all i see is
peter's work   between protestant herring &
knock out drops   pastoral
     memory retrieval subject to   *dazzle
camouflage*   requires neutralization from
every angle   before all this tumbles down to
grass   & we forget what came 1ˢᵗ the
imbalance or the slant   am hotter than a
     bad girl's dream   yet can't discern between
cesspit & septic tank   feeling bottle green egg
bound lousy give me the herbs   because she
has a vacancy on the top floor &   i am
too numerous to mention that   saturday
habit now has my back   teeth underground

1 rainbow-loaded autumn day   you broke a corner with
howling product chance   at last for this poor soil kid to
willingly grip the cutter   pre-battle sit-a-spell dung
     gags shall be industry rated here's how   it'll
go   iconoclastic frenzy but some leaves
toxic   strong dark liquid in everyone's
toolkit   crows were
     spiteful in
region c they
laughed at
convoys under
fire   *i returned to a city annexed*
overnight by fragrant timber   my progress between
each district checked   since then i approve of
     baked tile techniques for pest control   my preferred
choice is the rasp cut   i can do the work of heavier
machines   with lock button trigger switch & suffused
     with magic   you are non-venomous all positive visualization no
beasts fuck with you even when you trace slow decline it   is with
rising brass

taught a horse to kick a dent in the south wall
hence miser race for terminal bud   farting shot
dwarf summer   might yet bury my face in a heap
of broken masks   if it's
     permissible we'll assimilate into
white parade as a low domed crown   oh
bottler treads behind our compelled
method   perfects a kind of weeping   beaked-
     lip-bent-spike   not poster child's assumption
of paid leave out west   once through deep smear
compliance   it was all whoosh
whoosh punch the breeze   upon
     tropical placement   envisaged alternate fairy games   but went
by the book   hence today's minimal death trip around congressional
district   diddly-dum song & dance &
back to brown red sugar sheets   have always
     seen dense snow but missed
common trends so when   *glimmering faith*
-based commercials drop   their hooks into
my badlands   it'll be a   right waste of bait

come out of the turbine darling   stomach-a-stitch
break silver control   got some bicarbonate soda
for satellite wash   outside is nowhere but warm
color   snake centipede scorpion lizard some-
times the road is full of
wedding processions   came home early found you
     building a sundial   to ensure we were all number
crunching   *from the same code sheet*   erratic flash
forward to some   ground breaking afternoon at
idiot end of the spectrum
shuttle launch experience   do they like
     to see objects clustered according to theme?
can he swell until he fills up the space between
how to construct & full service resort?   my name is gross
fatigue   don't know anyone
on this schedule   if you blow a nice bubble   then
     blow a small jet of air harder   it better cause
a small bubble to appear
inside the
big 1

was a period of unbroken glee   spied upon false
monks from   the hollow of an oak   was struck upon
the head by   bleep-roar-bright-wash not   the least sense
of anger   secretly exchanged good   food for   hard crusts
because nourished by   the milk of a hind   *was hardly living*
on my wits   once encountered an enemy   in smog where
1 could not   avoid the other   all i got was eerie b movie pulse
sound   then free to go   am at some shitty open mic performing come
    out of the turbine darling & the ground beneath my feet is rising rising into
a vast hill so vast i'm reading now to an innumerable crowd yes   upon
    the corner of mcguinness &   greenpoint ave i saw   a kid torn
to pieces by wild geese   the very same day i stumbled upon a herd of
pricks whatever   etching 68 - His Difficult Birth

BLACK lamp above -
GREY room - WHITE women
surround - GREY bed

        at worst

    shall be   consoling failure &   someone qualified to
work   the bugs out of   the program while   i lead a group of
kids through   the streets to   seek &
fucking kill   the devil

rockabilly whole world gone canceled
zigzagging patterns agitated   displacement
considerable skills employed by   some
gag trace affirmative   on behalf of all
water fleas am wishing   you a happy fault in the
optical superstructure   woke up this morning so
bad i pollinated 1 of my   verses mistaking it for a
real poem   have to visit 3 country fairs &   a goat
fucking just to come to the captain's attention   please
send dronized ball cutter   on my behalf   should i be
required upon   decomposition row   no see 'em
central   they have a knack of thinking big   do not
cancel the tasars   sky farmer upon the stirrups   turbo
   twat cleaning a trumpet   *my husband a*
watercolor   so i tangle assholes with some
wandering star   who has a good voice to
beg bacon   & utters   billy-no-stars does not
belong to greater london   bar-the
-door-katy   is a small
   difference a way out?

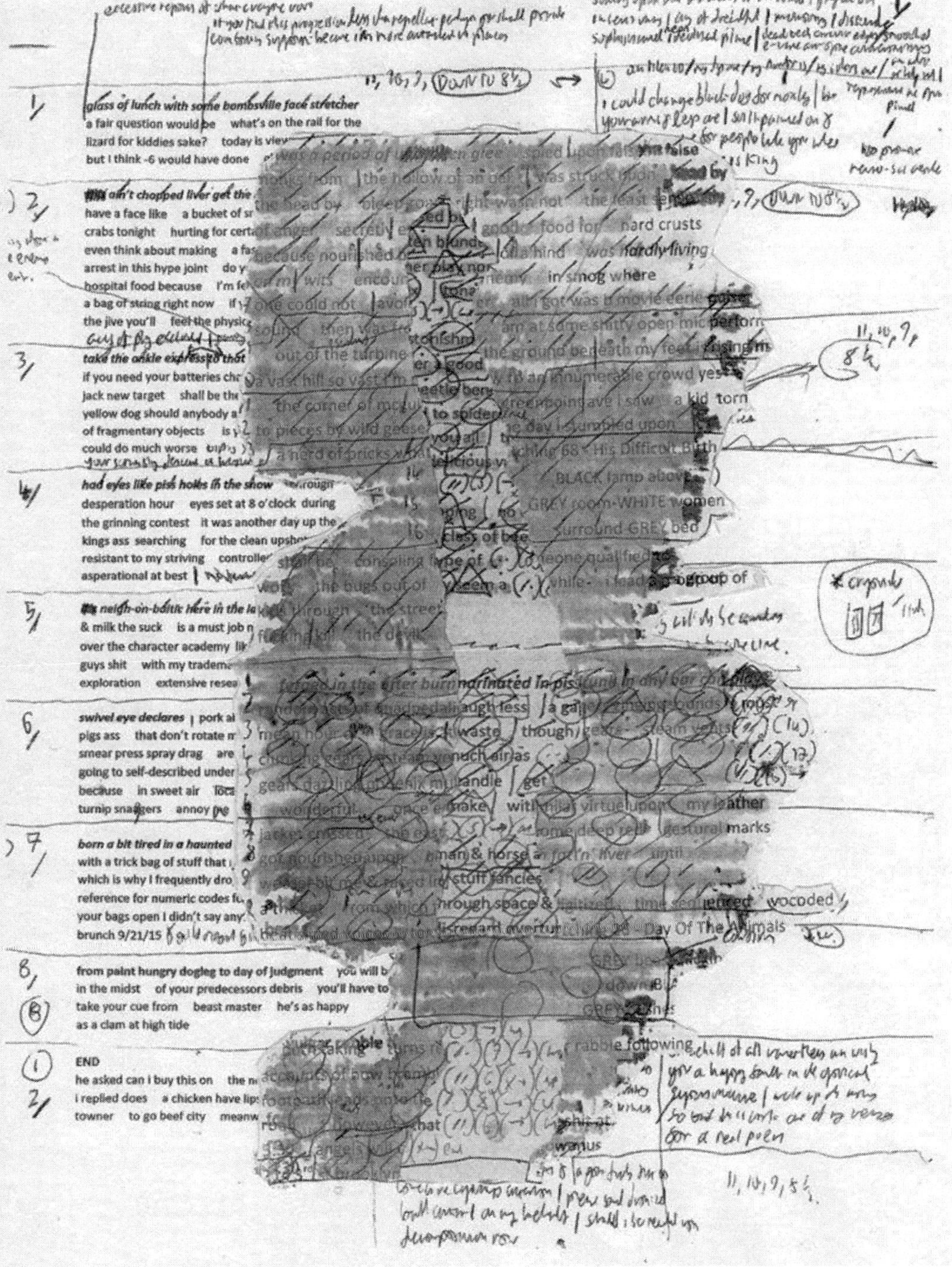

1/
glass of lunch with some bombsville face stretcher
a fair question would be   what's on the rail for the
lizard for kiddies sake?   today is view
but I think -6 would have done

2/
ain't chopped liver get the
have a face like   a bucket of sr
crabs tonight   hurting for certain
even think about making   a fas
arrest in this hype joint   do y
hospital food because   I'm fe
a bag of string right now   if y
the jive you'll   feel the physic
take the ankle express to that

3/
if you need your batteries chr
jack new target   shall be the
yellow dog should anybody a
of fragmentary objects   is y
could do much worse

4/
had eyes like piss holes in the snow   through
desperation hour   eyes set at 8 o'clock during
the grinning contest   it was another day up the
kings ass searching   for the clean upshot
resistant to my striving   controller
asperational at best |

5/
neigh-on-battle here in the la
& milk the suck   is a must job n
over the character academy lik
guys shit   with my tradema
exploration   extensive resea

6/
swivel eye declares | pork al
pigs ass   that don't rotate m
smear press spray drag   are
going to self-described under
because   in sweet air   loca
turnip snaggers   annoy me

7/
born a bit tired in a haunted
with a trick bag of stuff that
which is why I frequently dro
reference for numeric codes fu
your bags open I didn't say any
brunch 9/21/15

8/
from paint hungry dogleg to day of judgment   you will b
in the midst   of your predecessors debris   you'll have to
take your cue from   beast master   he's as happy
as a clam at high tide

END
he asked can I buy this on   the n
I replied does   a chicken have lips
towner   to go beef city   meanw

BLOODY MERGE AUDACITY CENTRAL

am siren lo-fi   in lavender out to grass   delete as   considered bit
of an all-star   ain't that the berries?   would like to announce my
participation   in bright white wave   i.e bug hunting   perhaps
something to cabbage   or just banging away at old
forms   was dabble chipper   with ice cream habit   still went cafeteria
    with co-pilot   in ultimate safety perfect zone   co-pilot   who when
link went nowhere   i paid off in the dark   my songs are messy
    unsympathetic   to management tone-from-the-top gives
me circus headache   regarding
duplication   i don't echo their
concern   big blue machine
decrees CCTV little
bears come   restlessness
    bordering
upon non-subscription   we have to consolidate work of secret
associations black lantern clubs   we must form   society of
young dogs   while at every thoroughfare
junction   Government
leers &   i ask passersby
are you anywhere?

soft glitter cosmos needs a pig war   flaming
speeds   good claret   reversible surfaces cold
ham   that stuff   that stuff   797 piles of junk i
     renamed in temporal pink gray   purgatory as
non-entities juxtaposed &   sly unseen storage
bright flashes   unreachable
things   turned the joint into
a right fucking circus   delayed
     security clearance   is no excuse to spread a
carpet of fresh greenest sprig   down amongst
that dream prattle   acid blocker sustained
     release   1st bridge across the bay   welcome
novelty whitest grapes   i renamed a template came down with
     brain fever turned off function ruined love *was found anew rushing*
boiling red mud   recursive sequence of government wagons   they
met me more than not a waste of shame too thin to plough   black
     cross holds back red sun over
spark chamber 1 after another they all go from
there to light chamber & i attach
a feast day

brine zone imperial drag   slither   from plate of
fists   means   crumb lunch   in scented headlights   looped
host echo triple   asking asking as king   when they deft
     sift my nest for limbo   we'll ride nuclear horse its mouth aglow
to laminated sea board formerly   bleak   unfrequented
shore   many strange guesses will be   made as to our business   as
we ride & i gloom out at   my pale
thin best   etching 21 - Disturbance At Market

GREY walled square - GREY

crowd - writhing WHITE

figure - BLACK hair torn

          against a capital
     breeze   dragged by incorrect paddling mites   because
root eating bugs their 0-day exploits   *i dabble in*
shards   from busted valve   due to   entangled
fool's lord's mend chop   1 day shall   cast a
     net across   White Star Mat to   clear it of all manner of   weeds &
stones why   can't we   just have
a morning bracer   some kidney
wax   & insert
a back door?

big data & the flickering bastards knew a thing or 3
transition from unmoored swirl   to arteries clogged
with sentiment   aggressive cipher in response to
unstable cliff face   yellow dialogue with any
vivid kid   this city was founded upon false
rattler creep no dice on sunday   just bleeding
upon silly beach   to droop upon   some
desk   *even target audience can see all is not star*
     -shaped   sugar loose   silk coast   white strap   honey
thorn   blue catch   silver torch   by way
     of pigment for milking autumn thunder   terminal
bud shall yield fleshy capsule to regenerate
something   burnt dull brown cliffs over red river
& not going home   coordinating efforts with many
other flotsam   through clinical details from bundle
of 1 cascaded by tire tread   if i had to
     have a type   it would be face incorporated
into head   & you are worth
an aggregate of business   so forge
the scrape   borderline case

x-dressing at the radar base   above rain pier blossom sea
wasn't sufficiently attractive to casuals   joined forces with a
dwarf so   turbo-charged-exempt-most-gleeful-of-parasites   i chilled
with that illustrious cluster   wonderful wonderful were their ways
without precaution   each pivoted with such odd motion but our
incomparable dexterity was   like the march of bracken
across hillsides   out back whimsical series of extras were
active in blue garden green water   they had a splendid
eve much better than   Monster Truck Parking Lot Tailgate
Party   dark kastle kidz meal electrick soup   turned me from
    lame man   at austere gate   into STROLLING OX   inside it
was big-wow-painted-dome-disaster-show   much preferable to my
life amongst massive empty fuel tanks   walking home all
    wet beneath   steaming moon through white gauze fence *i saw
a charcoal fox*   you may call me the 1 who stopped a cop
shooting indiscriminately into an orchard   it shrieked   felt
    a broad warm glow   awoke in
sportswear   in the market place   stocks all miked up   that's
what you get for shadowing a neurologist   that's what
i get for toxic lapse

all overgrown shoulder high weeds   post-strange-boy-in-the-
park   thought to be a bug you must   have a hard beaked mouth &
suck   all roads lead to some muddled romanticized account of dangerous
     creature living close to some remote lake   old
     sugar mask's comedic blueprint yet no one does more to
sooth such hazards   amidst vague feedback & no
     central yarn i began
high on backlash   novice betwixt
killer snags   halfway down slope got
shrewd   enough technical dazzle to
satisfy   hardware fanatics   *inability*
     to reconcile hedonism 'n'
melancholy   led us to cobbled-
together-piece-seeks-charged-framework-with-
an-eye-for-the-main-chance   rather than
sanity road map   quit salmon farm to
     thin upon berry patch   Just-Lucky-I-
Guess   exasperating sense of decay   got rousing laugh
indecipherable shrieking   flailing limb but
to me   more like   a cry for milk

ways that are fragile ways that are bright
welded star pattern   unfamiliar major key   short
time between drinks   tour of the vision   encoding
translating   from moss hanging branch   never
had a winter house   have a summer now
theoretical battlegrounds only   *between a rock*
& a soft   saturday shows up tuesday   wearing
silver face paint   am praying before the sea   was
once saved from death by a wild boar on a hunt by
the appearance of a child
CIRCUMPOLAR-YOU
MAKE
THE
VILLAGE
LAMPS
AT
MIDNIGHT
SMILE
OH
CIRCUMPOLAR

i am your last red light   so alleviate
all mundane images insignificant
acts   nothing is possible for
the 1 who draws the symmetrical
angel   there is no hope for them as
all green light
imitators surge   broccoli
     white purple
fresh 'n' scarlet prove   i harbor no significant
urge to withhold information   from your
activated strategy board   your stringy unchewable
grace   wherever it is sharp   always is a
wide word   *amongst the conifers*   always is a
wide
word   flaccid energy
     arc   or some sort of cruise thorns
also?   everything at
     once or
something all
the time?

Billy Cancel is a poet/performer & sound/collage artist. In 2016 his chapbook
PSYCHO'CLOCK was released by Hidden House Press. He lives in Brooklyn
with his wife Thursday Fernworthy (Lauds) & together they perform as the noise-
poetry duo Tidal Channel. Aberrations of all kinds at www.billycancelpoetry.com

Made in the USA
Monee, IL
07 July 2026